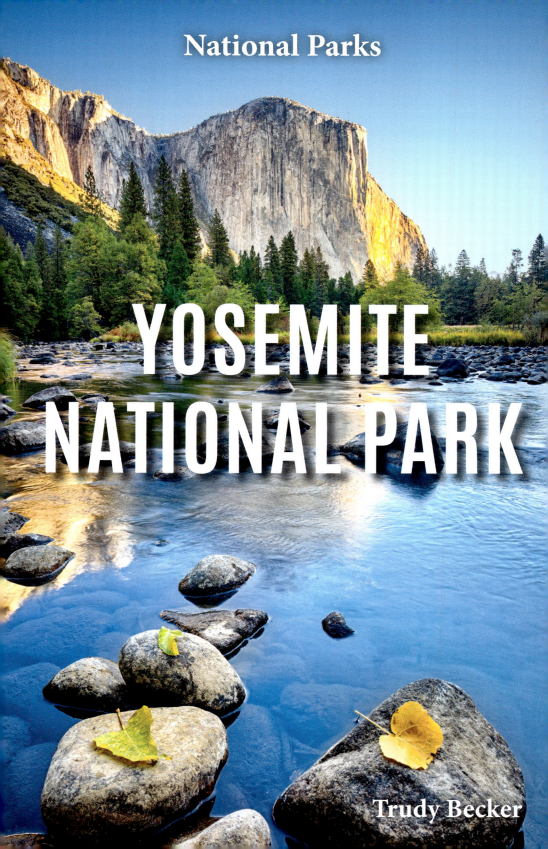

WWW.APEXEDITIONS.COM

Copyright © 2025 by Apex Editions, Mendota Heights, MN 55120. All rights reserved. No part of this book may be reproduced or utilized in any form or by any means without written permission from the publisher.

Apex is distributed by North Star Editions:
sales@northstareditions.com | 888-417-0195

Produced for Apex by Red Line Editorial.

Photographs ©: Shutterstock Images, cover, 1, 6–7, 10–11, 14–15, 20–21, 30–31, 34–35, 44–45, 50–51, 54–55; iStockphoto, 4–5, 8–9, 16–17, 19, 22–23, 32–33, 36–37, 39, 40–41, 42–43, 46–47, 56–57; Stevedunleavy.com/Moment/Getty Images, 12–13; Ralph H. Anderson/National Park Service, 24–25; Bettmann/Getty Images, 26–27; Ted Soqui/Corbis Historical/Getty Images, 28–29; Rebecca L. Latson/Moment/Getty Images, 48–49; Steve Bumgardner/Yosemite Conservancy/National Park Service/AP Images, 52–53; National Park Service, 58–59; Red Line Editorial, 59

Library of Congress Control Number: 2024943628

ISBN
979-8-89250-457-7 (hardcover)
979-8-89250-473-7 (paperback)
979-8-89250-504-8 (ebook pdf)
979-8-89250-489-8 (hosted ebook)

Printed in the United States of America
Mankato, MN
012025

NOTE TO PARENTS AND EDUCATORS

Apex books are designed to build literacy skills in striving readers. Exciting, high-interest content attracts and holds readers' attention. The text is carefully leveled to allow students to achieve success quickly.

TABLE OF CONTENTS

Chapter 1

SEEING THE VALLEY 5

Chapter 2

ALL ABOUT YOSEMITE 8

Natural Wonder

EL CAPITAN 18

Chapter 3

PEOPLE AND YOSEMITE 20

Chapter 4

FUN AT YOSEMITE 30

Natural Wonder

BRIDALVEIL FALL 38

Chapter 5

WILDLIFE 41

Chapter 6

SAVING YOSEMITE 51

PARK MAP • 58
COMPREHENSION QUESTIONS • 60
GLOSSARY • 62
TO LEARN MORE • 63
ABOUT THE AUTHOR • 63
INDEX • 64

The hike from Yosemite Valley to Glacier Point goes up 3,214 feet (980 m).

SEEING THE VALLEY

A hiker walks up a trail at Yosemite National Park. She passes mossy rocks. Trees and wildflowers line the path. She is heading toward Glacier Point.

The hiker rounds a corner. Suddenly, she sees Yosemite Falls. The water rushes down a cliff. The hiker keeps going. After a few miles, she reaches the viewpoint. The hiker looks out over Yosemite Valley. She spots Half Dome in the distance. She can't wait to hike more of the park.

The word *Yosemite* comes from a Miwok term for "grizzly bear."

FALLS HIGH AND LOW

Yosemite Falls is made of three connected waterfalls. Upper Yosemite Falls is the biggest. The water drops 1,430 feet (436 m). From some viewpoints, hikers can see all three parts.

Chapter 2

ALL ABOUT YOSEMITE

Yosemite National Park is in central California. The park is in the Sierra Nevada. This mountain range runs through much of the state. Yosemite National Park is huge. It covers almost 750,000 acres (304,000 ha). That's about the size of Rhode Island.

The Sierra Nevada range also goes into the state of Nevada.

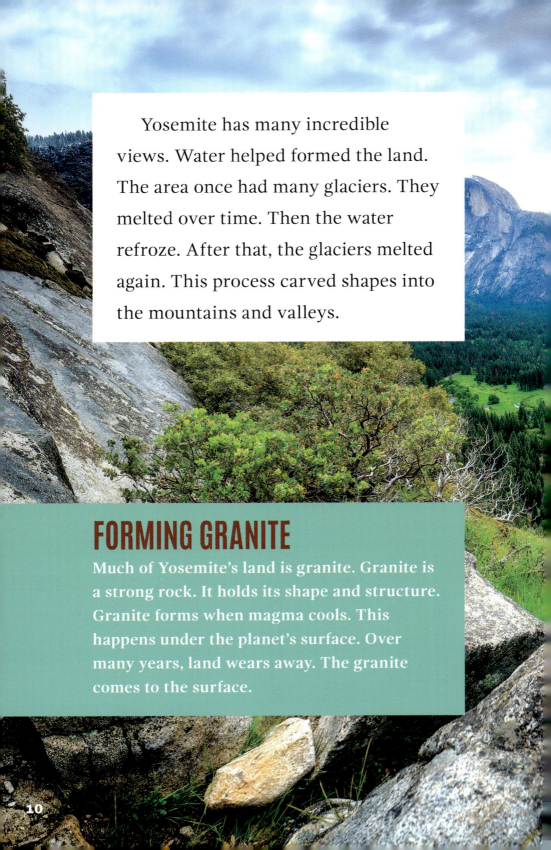

Yosemite has many incredible views. Water helped formed the land. The area once had many glaciers. They melted over time. Then the water refroze. After that, the glaciers melted again. This process carved shapes into the mountains and valleys.

FORMING GRANITE

Much of Yosemite's land is granite. Granite is a strong rock. It holds its shape and structure. Granite forms when magma cools. This happens under the planet's surface. Over many years, land wears away. The granite comes to the surface.

Granite in the Sierra Nevada can be between 120 and 185 million years old.

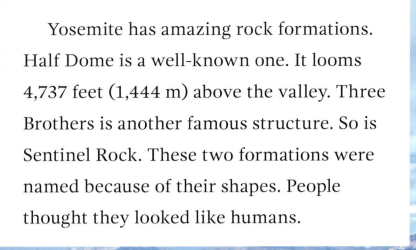

Yosemite has amazing rock formations. Half Dome is a well-known one. It looms 4,737 feet (1,444 m) above the valley. Three Brothers is another famous structure. So is Sentinel Rock. These two formations were named because of their shapes. People thought they looked like humans.

LIKE A CHURCH

In one spot, glaciers wore away the rock. The rock's shape became sharper and thinner. People said it looked like the top of a church. They used that to name the rock. They called it Cathedral Peak.

The hike to Cathedral Peak is 5.9 miles (9.5 km).

Yosemite is full of water. The Tuolumne and the Merced are the biggest rivers. They flow from high areas to low ones. The park also has several lakes. Yosemite is full of waterfalls, too. The falls flow all year. They are strongest in the springtime because of melting snow.

FIREFALL

Every February, Horsetail Fall does something special. The sun hits the water just right. It makes the water look orange. The sight looks like fire flowing down the cliff. People come from all around to see it.

Visitors need special permits to enter Yosemite during the Firefall.

Much of Yosemite is forested. That includes the famous groves of giant sequoia trees. Many sequoias grow in Mariposa Grove. These trees are huge. They are also ancient. Over time, these trees have survived storms and fires. They have also lived through changes to the land.

Some giant sequoias are more than 3,000 years old.

Natural Wonder

EL CAPITAN

El Capitan is iconic. It is one of Yosemite's most famous spots. El Capitan is a granite rock formation. The structure is very tall. It is three times higher than the Eiffel Tower. Visitors can see El Capitan from many areas. El Capitan Meadow is a common viewing spot.

El Capitan is famous for rock climbing. The climb is very difficult. The structure is not only tall. It is also steep. The sides are slippery. Even good climbers struggle with it.

> **El Capitan is 7,573 feet (2,308 m) tall. Several climbing routes lead to the top.**

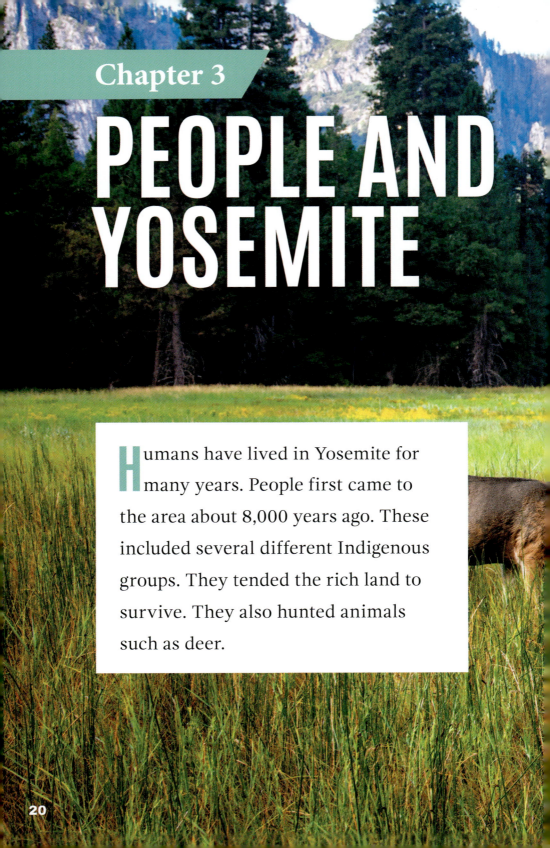

Chapter 3
PEOPLE AND YOSEMITE

Humans have lived in Yosemite for many years. People first came to the area about 8,000 years ago. These included several different Indigenous groups. They tended the rich land to survive. They also hunted animals such as deer.

Mule deer are common in Yosemite Valley.

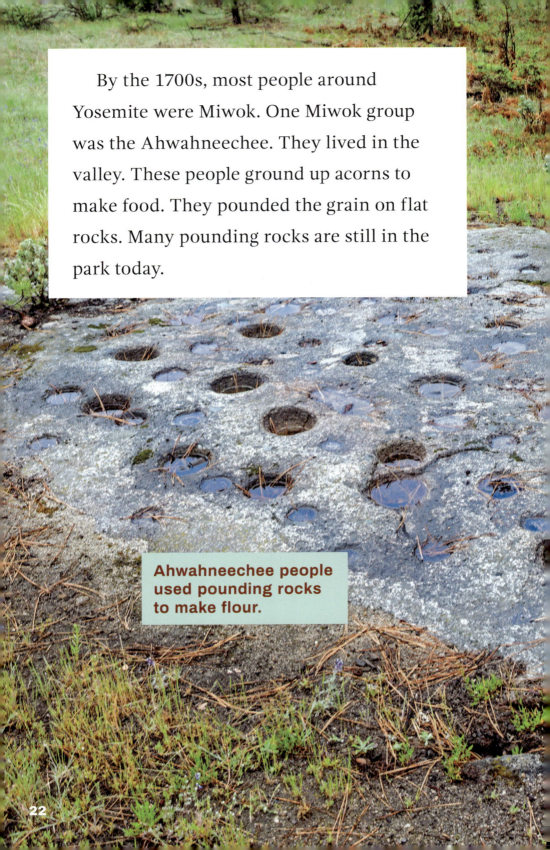

By the 1700s, most people around Yosemite were Miwok. One Miwok group was the Ahwahneechee. They lived in the valley. These people ground up acorns to make food. They pounded the grain on flat rocks. Many pounding rocks are still in the park today.

Ahwahneechee people used pounding rocks to make flour.

TWO BEAR CUBS

An old Miwok story tells about El Capitan. The Miwok call the stone Tutokanula. The name means "inchworm." In the story, two bear cubs climb the stone. It grows, and they get stuck. A worm helps save them.

Miwok people are known for basket weaving.

In the 1840s, the California Gold Rush began. Many white settlers moved to the area. They mined gold, hoping to get rich. But settlers often clashed with Indigenous people. The settlers pushed many Indigenous people out. Some Ahwahneechee people came back. But they no longer controlled their homelands.

Soon, business and tourism grew in the area. Authors, painters, and explorers also took interest in the land. John Muir was a naturalist. Muir and others tried to protect the land. Eventually, it worked. In 1864, President Abraham Lincoln signed a bill. It protected some of the land. Then, in 1890, Yosemite became a national park.

CHINESE IMMIGRANTS

In the late 1800s, many Chinese immigrants arrived in the area. They got jobs building camps and roads. They cooked for other workers, too. Many immigrants were treated badly. But they played a big role in developing Yosemite.

In 1903, President Theodore Roosevelt (left) met with John Muir at Yosemite National Park.

Today, some Miwok people work at the national park and teach visitors about their people's history.

In the 1900s, Yosemite grew into a modern park. People built places for visitors to stay. They also built roads. Tioga Pass opened to cars in 1919. Visitors increased slowly over time. By the 1960s, millions came each year. And by the 2020s, Yosemite was one of the most popular national parks.

MIWOK TODAY

White settlers pushed the Miwok people out of Yosemite in the early 1900s. But many Miwok returned. They still live near Yosemite today. The Miwok host a spring festival each year. Park visitors sometimes go to the festival.

Chapter 4

FUN AT YOSEMITE

Visitors come to see the park's beautiful sights. Many people camp. Some go backpacking in different areas. Visitors can also drive through the park. Roads lead to different outlooks. Valley Floor Loop is a popular road. It passes some of the park's most famous spots.

Campers at Yosemite can see thousands of stars at night.

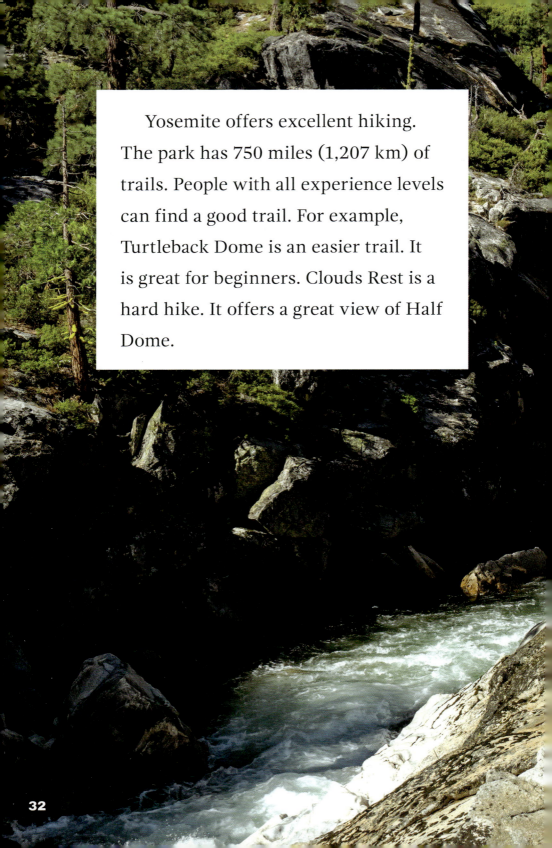

Yosemite offers excellent hiking. The park has 750 miles (1,207 km) of trails. People with all experience levels can find a good trail. For example, Turtleback Dome is an easier trail. It is great for beginners. Clouds Rest is a hard hike. It offers a great view of Half Dome.

Some hikes require equipment, such as hiking boots and backpacks.

To stay safe, people must wear life jackets while rafting.

Water activities are popular in summer. Visitors can swim in Merced River. They can swim in other bodies of water, too. Some people get licenses to fish. The water is also great for boating. Groups can raft down the rivers.

WINTER FUN

During winter, Yosemite hikers often use snowshoes. Others bring cross-country skis. These help people move across the land. The park also has areas to go downhill skiing or snowboarding.

Many visitors enjoy watching wildlife. Swan Lake is a great area for spotting birds. Trumpeter swans are the most famous. That is how the lake got its name. Visitors also watch for bigger wildlife. The meadows are a popular place for this activity. Over the seasons, many large mammals move through the meadows.

ON HORSEBACK

Some visitors explore the park on foot. Others go by car. One company even offers horseback riding. Visitors travel in a group. A guide leads the horses along the trails.

The trumpeter swan is the heaviest flying bird in North America. It can weigh more than 26 pounds (12 kg).

Natural Wonder

BRIDALVEIL FALL

Bridalveil Fall is in Yosemite Valley. This waterfall is easy to reach. Visitors can use Bridalveil Fall Trail. The path leads to a beautiful view of the waterfall. The water plunges 620 feet (189 m). The area is often windy and misty. This weather makes the water look like a wedding veil. That's how the waterfall got its name.

Bridalveil Fall flows year round. But it is strongest in the springtime. Visitors may even get splashed.

During winter, the trail to Bridalveil Fall becomes slippery as the water freezes.

Coyotes are common in Yosemite National Park.

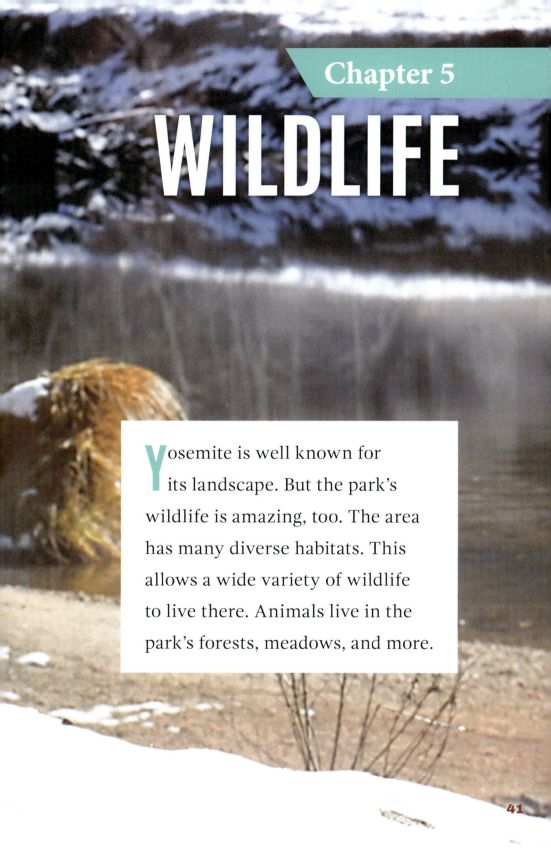

Chapter 5
WILDLIFE

Yosemite is well known for its landscape. But the park's wildlife is amazing, too. The area has many diverse habitats. This allows a wide variety of wildlife to live there. Animals live in the park's forests, meadows, and more.

More than 90 kinds of mammals live in Yosemite. Some are huge predators. For example, mountain lions move through mountainous areas. Black bears make their homes in the forests. Some Yosemite mammals are rare. Fewer than 40 Sierra Nevada red foxes have been spotted.

Between 300 and 500 black bears live in Yosemite National Park.

BIG BATS

Yosemite is home to many kinds of bats. One example is western mastiffs. They are the largest bats in North America. Their wings can stretch 22 inches (56 cm). During the day, the bats sleep in rocky caves. At night, they go out to eat insects.

Steller's jays eat mostly nuts, seeds, and insects.

More than 250 types of birds live in Yosemite. Some stay the whole year. Others fly through on their way to other areas. Steller's jays and American robins are two common birds. Mountain chickadees are another. They live in the park's forest areas.

HUGE BIRDS

Great gray owls are some of Yosemite's biggest birds. Peregrine falcons are another. Both are fierce hunters. They feed on small rodents. So do bald eagles and golden eagles.

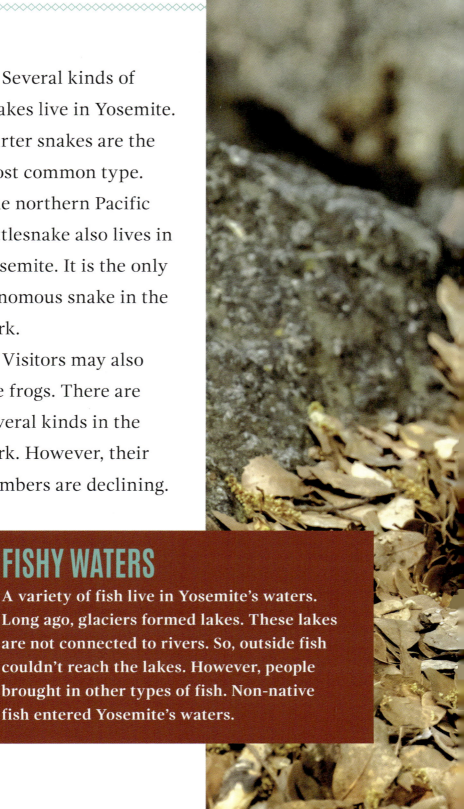

Several kinds of snakes live in Yosemite. Garter snakes are the most common type. The northern Pacific rattlesnake also lives in Yosemite. It is the only venomous snake in the park.

Visitors may also see frogs. There are several kinds in the park. However, their numbers are declining.

FISHY WATERS

A variety of fish live in Yosemite's waters. Long ago, glaciers formed lakes. These lakes are not connected to rivers. So, outside fish couldn't reach the lakes. However, people brought in other types of fish. Non-native fish entered Yosemite's waters.

Rattlesnakes use their tongues to smell.

47

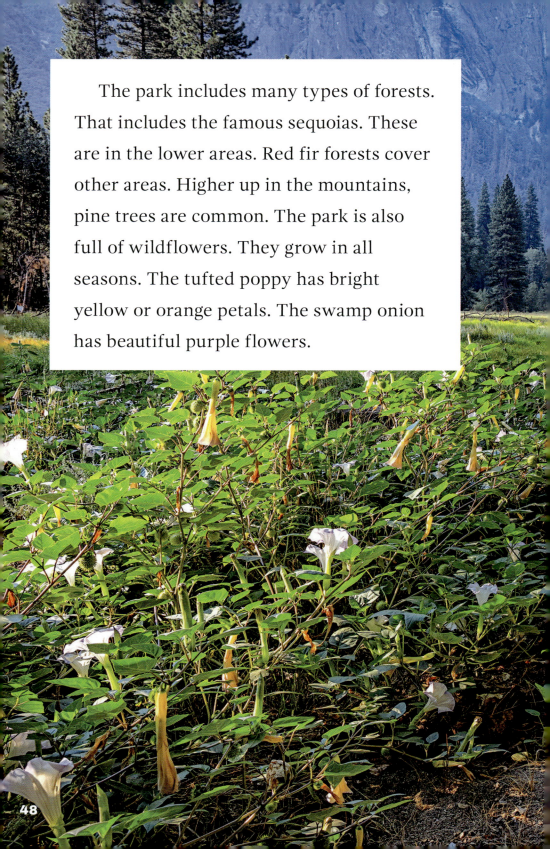

The park includes many types of forests. That includes the famous sequoias. These are in the lower areas. Red fir forests cover other areas. Higher up in the mountains, pine trees are common. The park is also full of wildflowers. They grow in all seasons. The tufted poppy has bright yellow or orange petals. The swamp onion has beautiful purple flowers.

A field of datura wildflowers bloom in Yosemite Valley.

Lyell Glacier (above) is one of two glaciers within Yosemite National Park.

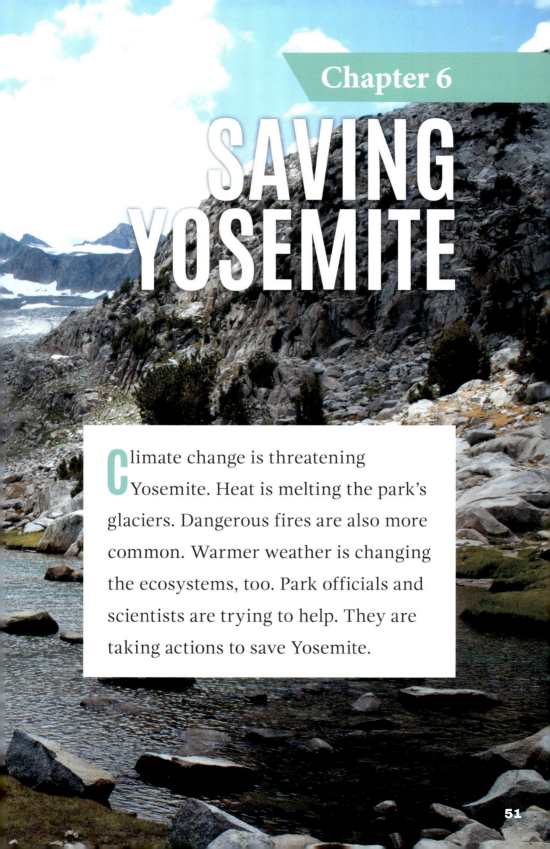

Chapter 6

SAVING YOSEMITE

Climate change is threatening Yosemite. Heat is melting the park's glaciers. Dangerous fires are also more common. Warmer weather is changing the ecosystems, too. Park officials and scientists are trying to help. They are taking actions to save Yosemite.

Some projects focus on wildlife populations. In the past, people hunted too many bighorn sheep. Many died from diseases, too. But in the 1980s, people brought in more sheep. The population recovered. Invasive species threaten the park, too. Mud snails started taking over Yosemite's waters. Park workers try to stop them from spreading.

SAVING THE FROG
The California red-legged frog lives in Yosemite. It is the largest native frog in the western United States. For 50 years, there were no red-legged frogs in the park. But people brought them back in 2017. Now, workers carefully track their population.

Workers release bighorn sheep into the wild in 2015.

Other projects focus on Yosemite's landscapes. Buildings, trails, and invasive plants hurt the wetlands. Workers took out some invasive plants. They built a safe path through wetland areas. And they planted new plants.

Park workers have found more than 250 kinds of invasive plants, including yellow star thistle.

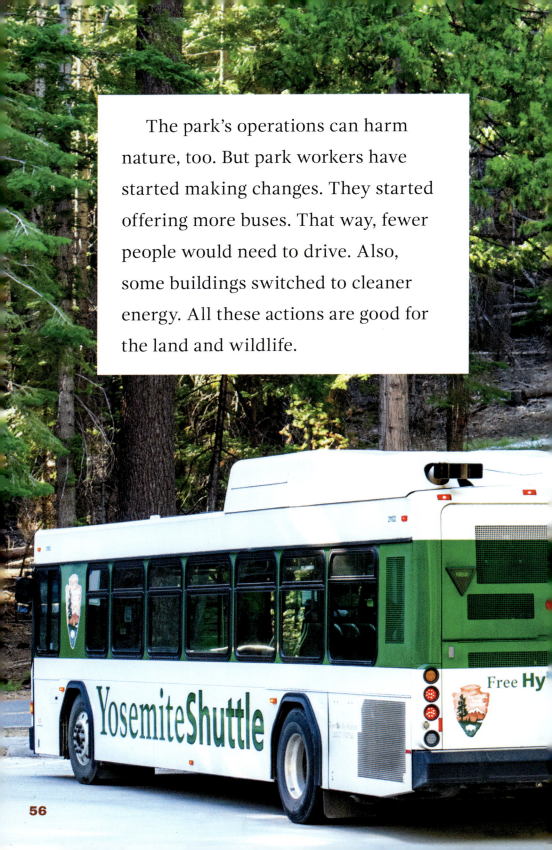

The park's operations can harm nature, too. But park workers have started making changes. They started offering more buses. That way, fewer people would need to drive. Also, some buildings switched to cleaner energy. All these actions are good for the land and wildlife.

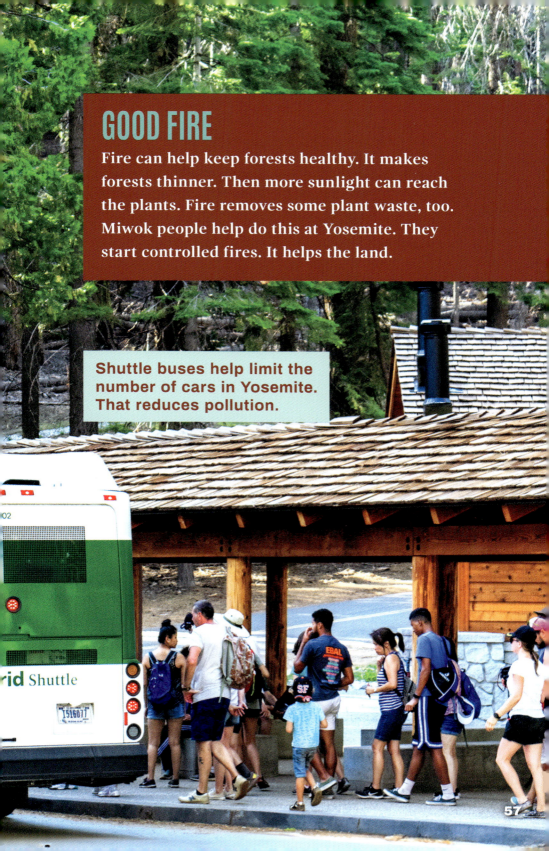

GOOD FIRE

Fire can help keep forests healthy. It makes forests thinner. Then more sunlight can reach the plants. Fire removes some plant waste, too. Miwok people help do this at Yosemite. They start controlled fires. It helps the land.

Shuttle buses help limit the number of cars in Yosemite. That reduces pollution.

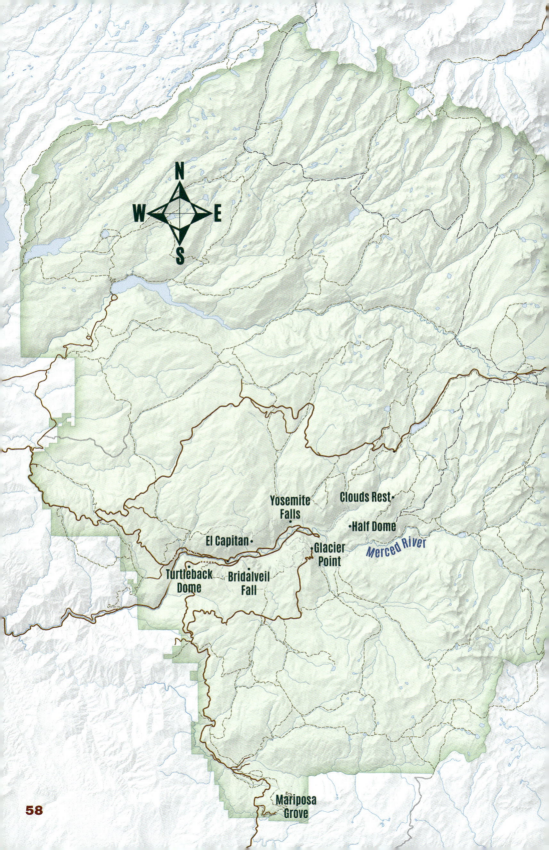

PARK MAP

COMPREHENSION QUESTIONS

Write your answers on a separate piece of paper.

1. Write a few sentences explaining the main ideas of Chapter 6.

2. If you visited Yosemite, what would you be most excited to see? Why?

3. Which hiking trail is good for beginners?
   - A. Half Dome
   - B. Turtleback Dome
   - C. Clouds Rest

4. How is climate change harming Yosemite National Park?
   - A. Bighorn sheep are more common.
   - B. Dangerous fires are more common.
   - C. Shuttle buses are more common.

5. What does **iconic** mean in this book?

*El Capitan is **iconic**. It is one of Yosemite's most famous spots. El Capitan is a granite rock formation.*

    A. high above the ground
    B. difficult to climb
    C. very well known

6. What does **diverse** mean in this book?

*The area has many **diverse** habitats. This allows a wide variety of wildlife to live there. Animals live in the park's forests, meadows, and more.*

    A. very different
    B. all the same
    C. extremely dangerous

Answer key on page 64.

GLOSSARY

climate change
A dangerous long-term change in Earth's temperature and weather patterns.

ecosystems
Groups of living things and their environments.

glaciers
Large, slow-moving bodies of ice.

groves
Small groups of trees.

habitats
The places where plants or animals normally live.

immigrants
People who move to a new country.

Indigenous
Related to the original people who lived in an area.

invasive
Spreading quickly in a new area and causing many problems there.

mammals
Animals that have hair and produce milk for their young.

native
Originally living in an area.

naturalist
A person who studies nature.

venomous
When animals use a poison to bite or sting prey.

TO LEARN MORE

BOOKS

Gagliardi, Sue. *California Wildfires*. Mendota
Heights, MN: Focus Readers, 2020.
Leaf, Christina. *Yosemite National Park*.
Minneapolis: Bellwether Media, 2023.
Sebra, Richard. *California*. Minneapolis: Abdo
Publishing, 2023.

ONLINE RESOURCES

Visit **www.apexeditions.com** to find links and
resources related to this title.

ABOUT THE AUTHOR

Trudy Becker lives in Minneapolis, Minnesota.
She likes exploring new places and loves anything
involving books.

INDEX

Ahwahneechee people, 22, 25

backpacking, 30
bats, 43
birds, 36, 45

camping, 30
Cathedral Peak, 12
Chinese immigrants, 26
climate change, 51
Clouds Rest, 32

El Capitan, 18, 23

forests, 16, 41–42, 45, 48, 57
frogs, 46, 52

giant sequoia trees, 16, 48
Glacier Point, 5
glaciers, 10, 12, 46, 51
granite, 10, 18

Half Dome, 6, 12, 32
hiking, 5–7, 32, 35

Indigenous peoples, 20, 25
invasive species, 52, 55

Lincoln, Abraham, 26

Miwok people, 22–23, 25, 29, 57
Muir, John, 26

rock climbing, 18

Sentinel Rock, 12
Sierra Nevada, 8, 42
snakes, 46
Swan Lake, 36

Three Brothers, 12
trails, 5, 32, 36, 38, 55
Turtleback Dome, 32

water activities, 35
waterfalls, 6–7, 14, 38
white settlers, 25, 29
wildflowers, 5, 48
wildlife, 36, 41–43, 45–46, 48, 52, 56

ANSWER KEY:

1. Answers will vary; 2. Answers will vary; 3. B; 4. B; 5. C; 6. A